MW00413445

What Can You Expect When You Are Expecting A Puppy

What Can You Expect When You Are Expecting A Puppy

—ɯ—

Michael Schaier

Copyright © 2015 Michael Schaier CPDT-KA, ABC-DT, AKC-CGC Evaluator
All rights reserved.

ISBN: 1502880415
ISBN 13: 9781502880413

I am dedicating this book to Clarence and Rosie with gratitude for all the years we've spent together and the love we've shared. I will see you further up the road....

"Dogs, lives are short, too short, but you know that going in. You know the pain is coming, you're going to lose a dog, and there's going to be great anguish, so you live fully in the moment with her, never fail to share her joy or delight in her innocence, because you can't support the illusion that a dog can be your lifelong companion. There's such beauty in the hard honesty of that, in accepting and giving love while always aware that it comes with an unbearable price. Maybe loving dogs is a way we do penance for all the other illusions we allow ourselves and the mistakes we make because of those illusions." – Dean Koontz

Introduction

I would like to risk the assumption that the reason you picked up this book is because you are thinking about getting a puppy! CONGRATS… on getting a puppy not picking up the book. It never fails to amaze me how dogs convey utter love, devotion, and loyalty to their humans, no questions asked. They don't care about your race or religion, whether you are rich or poor, married or not! Your dog invariably will wrap himself around your heart and into your life. No agenda, no ulterior motives; just an endless supply of adoration and faithfulness. (And wet sloppy kisses, lots and lots of wet sloppy kisses!)

I truly believe the world would be a much better place if everyone experienced the love of a dog. They make us kinder, more compassionate humans. However, like most things in life this harmonious give and take love affair between dogs and us doesn't come without challenges; and this challenge is often called PUPPYHOOD.

As a professional dog trainer, I am fortunate to be able to engage in my passion on a full time basis. Being able to help bridge the communication gaps between man's best friend and man himself is humbling to say the least. A large portion of my students are puppies. Which means, an even larger portion of my human clientele are puppy mommies and daddies. Many of my clients are ones that acquire a puppy, get home, and then say, " What do I do now?"

Like any new parent, they usually are in a state of confusion and panic by the time they have reached out to me. Well meaning family and friends, fellow dog owners, their vet and/or a breeder have kindly (and sometimes not so kindly) offered their two cents on what they should be doing. Should they crate their puppy or not? Should they use a Wee Wee pad or strictly outdoor potty training? How will they get their newest family member to interact with their human siblings or for that matter older canine ones? All that contradictory "good" advice and intentions seem to go out the window as soon as this cuddly, warm ball of fur gets home. The tired, baffled and concerned new parents are left scratching their heads instead of their new best friend's belly.

I am more than just a Dog Trainer. I like to think of myself as a New Puppy Parent Teacher, for you will see it is you, the Mommy and Daddy, who really need to be trained.

I am also a straightforward, hardworking guy who knows a thing or two (or three or four) about dogs, especially puppies. This book is a compilation of all those things as well as my first hand experiences and years of hearing the same questions asked over and over again. It will give you some guidelines on what to expect from your new "BABY" and help you get through the first year of his puppy life. I also offer you easy to use right away training tips and a lot of laughs along the way, because as every new parent knows, laughter does make things better!

What makes this book even more helpful and different from the rest (besides my wit of course) is that I end each chapter with a little summary and a place to write notes that will make it easy to refer back to when you need it most. This book also will serve as a Puppy Scrapbook where you can use the blank spaces to journal all those PUPPY FIRSTS that happen along the way.

I'm not going to lie to you, its not going to be a walk in the park. Some days you yourself are going to feel like a dog, others you may feel like the hydrant! But on those trying days remember this quote: "In order to really enjoy a dog, one doesn't merely try to train him to be semi-human. The point of it is to open oneself to the possibility of becoming partly a dog." - Edward Hoagland

So roll over FIDO, no playing dead... we got a game of fetch to play here! In other words... lets begin!

Chapter One
So You Think Your Ready For A Puppy?

Getting a puppy is a decision that is going to affect the next couple of decades of your life. Kind of makes you stop and think for a second when I put it like that doesn't it? Good! The decision to get a puppy should not be taken lightly.

While impulse buying can be great under certain circumstances; this decision requires a little more consideration than say whether or not to purchase the Altoids or the Winter Fresh Tic Tacs in the grocery store checkout line. Yet, very few people really take the time to do any research on what type of puppy to get and this can be a recipe for disaster. Here's an example of getting a puppy without any planning.

I received a phone call from a nice sounding but frantic woman who had heard about me and wanted to discuss some training for her puppy. It seems her newly acquired friend was destroying her house. YIKES! So I told her I would come over for an evaluation.

When I arrived at her home, I found this adorable 70-something year old woman sitting on a couch holding the collar of her barking and overly outgoing 60 lb. gorgeous and extremely muscular pit bull puppy. This frisky canine had ripped up the sofa she was sitting on, shredded newspapers, and chewed holes in the kitchen walls! No kidding, actual holes! While it was obvious that the woman loved her dog, she just could not physically handle him. This breed of dog needs someone who is, for lack of a better way of saying this, a little more active. Clearly, this was a decision made totally from the heart without any thought to the consequences.

This was not a bad dog, he was just a friendly lad who had a whole lot of energy and we needed to figure out a way to get the steam out of this boy and we needed to do it quickly while she still had at least one cushion left to sit on! I explained a large part of our working together would involve long walks and maybe some play dates with other age and size appropriate puppies. The good news is my client and student (who is now a well adaptive and happy adult dog)

weathered this period and they are now best friends and companions for life.

While this story has a happy ending, not all of the ones I have encountered do. I cannot say it enough... do your homework.

I know you are so excited about this and just can't wait... so I am offering you some Cliffs Notes!

I can't begin to count the number of clients I have seen that never stop to contemplate how Rover really fits into their lives. This thinking ahead can save you the stress and anguish of finding out your puppy doesn't fit and now you are faced with the unthinkable nightmare of having to re-home your puppy or at the very least buy a new sofa like the woman in the story above.

Now is the time to ask yourself some really good questions. Are you a homeowner or are you renting? If you rent does your lease allow dogs? If so are there restrictions to size or weight? Do you have allergies? Do you have children? Are you planning on having any in the next 15-20 years? Are you able to afford the extra cost of a dog? Puppies aren't cheap! These are just a few of the questions you should be asking before you allow yourself to fall in love with that cute little fur ball. At the end of this chapter there is a fun (purely for entertainment) quiz that will get you thinking even more about your lifestyle and how, or if, a puppy would fit into it.

Does Size Really Matter?

Contrary to what many might believe... size doesn't really matter! But not in the way you may think! (Come on now this is a family book, geez.) The common mistake most folks make is assuming that a small breed puppy is better suited for apartment and that a large breed is right for a house with a huge backyard. Not true. Some of the best apartment dogs are Great Danes, and um, for the record, these dogs are not small!!! **Energy level is a much more important factor than size** (and yeah, I bolded that because it's an important thing you need to remember!).

Let me tell you about one of my clients who just so happened to live in an apartment and her unique problem she had with her small Jack Russell terrier. It seemed her little guy loved doing laps around the room. While running around in circles may not sound so strange, this tiny terror had a rather unusual way to unwind; his teeny weeny paws never touched the floor. He would do his running from couch to loveseat, windowsill to a chair, coffee table to ottoman. He never hit the ground! He may have been small in frame but this pint-sized fella had enough energy to fuel a nuclear power plant. A backyard or a few long walks a day would have helped. See, energy level is a much better factor when deciding then size!

On Your Mark, Get Set, GO SPOT GO!

We typically classify dogs into low, medium, and high energy. If you're into an active athletic lifestyle, a high-energy dog might be the right fit for you. If you tend to be more of the TV couch potato consider one of the low energy breeds. Do your research so when you pick out your puppy you will have a clearer picture as to how he will behave.

But remember…all puppies have high energy. Excess puppy energy is the biggest cause of puppy mayhem. Biting, nipping, jumping, digging, barking, etc. can all be attributed, to some extent, to excessive energy. Your biggest challenge as a puppy owner will be to reduce that energy and channel it into positive behavior patterns.

A great mantra for you to live by is:

"A tired (insert your puppy's name here) is a happy (insert your puppy's name here). And a tired (insert your puppy's name here) doesn't nip, jump and chew on the furniture nearly as much as one that is all revved up and rarin' to go."

Many clients tell me "Michael, I don't understand. I let my dog out into the backyard for lengthy periods of time and he's still chewing on my living room curtains." And I tell them, "Maybe he doesn't like the colors!" Nah just kidding. What I do tell them is that exercising your dog is not letting them into the yard by themselves and expecting them to run themselves into a state of exhaustion. For the most part, dogs are lazy. Seriously there is a reason why they are man's best friend you know. They are couch potatoes perfectly willing to watch Monday night football with you.

Like most of us, young dogs have got to be pushed to exercise. Throwing a ball, playing catch with a Frisbee, and taking Fido for a walk are all great ways to ensure your puppy gets the exercise he needs. And, ummm, not that I am saying you need it or anything, but it could help with that football watching beer belly you may have developed too.

Mars vs. Venus

Yes we have all heard it before, men are from Mars and Woman are from Venus, we are different, yadda yadda yadda. While gender seems to matter a lot in our two-legged world, I am not so sure it is all that important in the 4-legged one. Whether or not to get a boy or girl puppy is strictly a personal decision. Some people feel that female dogs are easier to train. Obviously, as a male dog trainer I can't say I agree with this! Also, it has been said that males tend to roam more than females. Is this possible, sure, but not a rule of thumb. The only things in regards to gender that are definite are the following:

1. Females tend to be smaller than males in most breeds of dogs.
2. If you want to breed your dog and have puppies, well then obviously your decision is made.

I need to get on my soapbox here for a minute and get a bit more serious. Please think long and hard before making the decision to breed. There are so many dogs looking to be adopted that are in shelters currently. More unwanted dogs are definitely not needed.

As mentioned earlier, all decisions as to what type of puppy you get are yours to make and it would be presumptuous of me to suggest one type over the other. That said, and since I am still on my soapbox, if you are still not sure between adoption vs. purchase of a pure breed, please consider the puppy up for adoption at your local shelter. These dogs all need homes with loving families and they make awesome companions. Okay stepping off the box now.

Are You Ready For A Dog Quiz

So by now you may be thinking, "I'm READY!" But are you really? I put together this fun quiz to see just how ready you really are. While this quiz is really just to make you smile, there are some very real truths you may not have thought about that it points out. So take it for fun, but do stop and think about how you would really answer them and why?

1. **How would you best describe your home where you live?**
   A. Cluttered and filled to capacity with stuff. Plus no storage area.
   B. I live in an apartment building that has a strong no pet policy.
   C. I can and plan to puppy proof my house to the best of my ability.

2. **Ten years from now I imagine my life will be like...**
   A. Who knows? I plan on traveling a lot in the next few years to find myself.

B. Good question. I'm moving out of the area.

C. I expect my life to continue pretty much the way it is now. But if something comes my way, I'm ready.

3. How would you be affected if your dog needed surgery or special medical care that would cost in excess of $500 and you did not have insurance?

A. Oh boy, that's a problem!

B. It would put a severe strain on my finances.

C. While money certainly doesn't grow on trees for us, we would do what we needed to do to get our pooch better; after all he is part of our family.

4. Who will watch your dog when you go out of town?

A. Never thought about it.

B. You mean someone has to watch it?

C. My sister (neighbor, friend, etc.) has offered to watch him while we are away and if they can't we know a really good PET HOTEL we can board him for the few days.

5. Which answer most closely describes why you want to get a dog?

A. Great chick or guy magnet.

B. Someone to play with after I get home from a long night of partying or a long day at the office.

C. A dog would be a loving addition to my life and our family.

Answers

If you answered mostly...

A- Maybe...NOT!

You think you want a dog, BUT, you may be in love with the idea more than the real thing! It may be best to re-evaluate WHY you want a dog.

B- You should really think this through...

Although you may feel strongly about getting a dog, stop and reconsider. Seriously like really, really, reconsider!

C- You're ready...

You have the right attitude for being a dog owner. You understand the responsibility entailed with a dog. You are ready to make a lifelong commitment to your pet. You want your dog to become a loving member of your family. You are prepared for all of the work it will require and for all of the surprises that may occur.

Chapter One Summary

- Getting a dog means making a 15-20 year commitment
- Don't be impulsive... DO YOUR HOMEWORK
- Keep in mind your lifestyle when researching dogs
- Energy level matters more than size of the dog
- Consider adopting a dog from a local shelter rather than a breeder

NOTES:

OUR PUPPY JOURNAL

We knew we were ready to get a puppy because:

_____

_____

_____

_____

We consider these types of breeds of dogs when we started doing our research:

_____

_____

_____

_____

We decided that _____ breed was the right choice for us because: _____

_____

_____

_____

_____

(Paste Pictures of Puppy here)

Chapter Two
So You're Getting A Puppy...

Way to go! You did your research and have decided what breed of dog suits your lifestyle best. You took our little quiz in Chapter One and found out that now is the perfect time to invite a four-legged companion into your life and heart. In other words, YOU ARE READY!

I know you are excited, who can blame you? However, a few things first.

Before you can bring home that little (or perhaps not so little) bundle of fur, you need to make sure your house is puppy proofed, that you understand what your puppy has and is going through and that you have a clear picture of what to expect from your new best friend. Lets consider this chapter to be your Puppy Basic Training!

Puppy Growth and Development from birth to 2 months.

Before we go any further we need to talk about the ABC's of puppies. A dog is considered a puppy from birth to one year of age and will go through many developmental stages during that period. Smaller dogs tend to mature earlier while larger breeds do not reach full maturity until they are approximately two years old. Rate of development can also vary depending on the breed.

Regardless of breed or size, all puppies are totally dependent on their mothers at birth. Puppies are born deaf, blind and toothless. They are unable to regulate their body temperature and cannot "eliminate" on their own. Puppies rely on their mothers and littermates for warmth. Unable to support their own weight, the newborns will paddle around on their front legs and pile into cozy heaps; it's a natural instinct that they have to conserve body temperature. When a young pup grows too cold he will quickly cry out to his mama for warmth.

Puppies are also dependent on their mothers for food. While they are born deaf and blind, they do have a strong sense of smell. From birth puppies use touch and smell to find their mothers. The first milk produced contains antibodies that help protect the puppies from disease during the early weeks of life. A newborn puppy will spend most of its time sleeping only waking to nurse.

Between three to seven weeks puppies are learning behavioral patterns that are specific to dogs. They are learning body posture and canine communication. It's during this time that interrelationships increase and they develop bonds that will stay with them for the rest of their lives. They learn how to inhibit their bite when romping with littermates and this is an important life lesson that will affect future behavior.

So when is the best time to get your dog then? If possible, try never to purchase a puppy that is less than eight weeks old. Eight to twelve weeks is considered the main socialization stage for puppies. It's the phase when they are really starting to interact with the rest of the pack and it is the perfect time to introduce the puppy to a new environment and a new family.

I often get calls from new dog owners desperate for help with very young puppies. It seems that their pups are biting harder than they should, lack social skills and tend to be more aggressive with other dogs. Often a dog suffering from these symptoms was removed from the litter too soon.

Sleeping Arrangements and Potty Training (see training tip at end of chapter for sample schedule)

While you are waiting for your puppy to be less dependent on his canine mama, there are plenty of things you can be doing.

Just like human parents must baby proof the house, you should puppy proof your house! The purpose of puppy proofing is to make sure you remove anything that could be harmful to your new pet such as cleaning products, electric cords or breakable glass. It's also a great way to make sure that possible items that may make appealing teething rings and chew toys are put away out of puppy's reach. If there are children in the home, removing favorite stuffed animals and their toys might be a very good idea as puppy may not be able to distinguish between his play items and theirs.

As you go through your home also keep in mind where your dog will sleep. Most new dog owners use a crate in the beginning; but there're still a few owners that I see that feel that crating a dog is inhumane or constitutes a negative situation. Here is my take on crating.

Crating the puppy creates a soft warm home and prevents your puppy from engaging in destructive behavior while not being watched. It's also an extremely important tool in potty training. That goes for either training your dog to go to the bathroom outside or using Wee-Wee pads in the house.

When getting a crate, make sure you purchase one that is the right size. The rule of thumb is the crate should be one and a half times your puppy's body length not including the tail. Crates come with dividers. You can make a large crate smaller and then gradually expand your puppies living quarters. The concept behind the dividers is that dogs are notoriously clean animals. By keeping puppy in an enclosed area he will do his best not to go to the bathroom and soil himself or his bed. In other words, when you come down in the morning to let your puppy out, his bladder is full from holding it in all night. Now you can then take him over to his bathroom area (be it outside or Wee-Wee pad), he relieves himself, you go crazy, give him a treat and tell him what a smart, wonderful doggie he is. Bada Bing Bada Boom... before you know it Puppy is trained! At least that is the concept.

Basic Supplies You Will Need
The list below is a good start of all the things you should have before bringing home your pooch. This is just a starting point and by no means everything you will need.

1. Leash and collar

2. Dog (puppy) food, training treats and water dishes
3. Training crate
4. Dog bed
5. Puppy appropriate sized stuffed toys and puppy safe chewing toys
6. Puppy gate to confine the puppy to certain area
7. ID tag
8. Grooming supplies (puppy safe shampoo, brush, etc.)

What to Expect those First Few Days

Puppies usually come home and are calm and quiet. They also are usually confused and bewildered by the change in their environment. As their confidence grows, their true personality starts to emerge. As that occurs, usually within the first month you have had them, all the typical puppy "issues" start to show itself like nipping, chewing, biting, jumping and so on. It's important to remember that every puppy ever born nips! Every puppy chews and every puppy play growls. Why? Because they are puppies, it's what they do!

I recently got a phone call from someone who heard about me and wanted to get some information about my dog training. After speaking for a little while, this nice woman informed me that while she enjoyed our conversation, she really did not think she would need my services. She went on to inform me that her 10-week-old Goldendoodle puppy, whom she had for a grand total of 3 days, was so good and calm as can be. Now you must understand that in the world of dog training, Goldendoodles are known as high-energy dogs. With this in mind, I suggested to this nice and perhaps a bit clueless woman that she might want to hold onto my number, just in case anything changes. I wished her luck and went about my own business. Three weeks later, I received a call from the same lady. Her phone call began with "HELP!" My point is, your puppy won't show his true puppy personality for a good 2-3 weeks after you bring him home.

Reminder: Puppies are not born with a manual that shows them how to "behave" in our world. It is our job to teach them what is acceptable versus what isn't. Just think if positions were reversed and we lived in a dog's world, instead of shaking hands or hugging, we would need to learn to jump on and lick whomever we were greeting. So my first and most important training tip for you is...

Don't expect your new puppy to understand what you want automatically! It takes work, patience, and consistency on our part.

Michael's Training Tip One

Usually, the first thing a new puppy parent calls me about is potty training. First thing to realize is (as with all of dog training) patience and consistency are the two key words to success. Dogs love a set routine and schedule. That's where the use of the crate coupled with feeding your puppy on a schedule will produce the results you're looking for.

Note: You should start off putting your puppy's food down and picking up the bowl approximately 30 minutes later. That way, your puppy learns to eat on your schedule, helping to increase the likelihood of " doing his business" 20-30 minutes after eating.

Sample Schedule

7:00 am – Potty. Go downstairs and take your puppy out of the crate. Immediately go with him outside or to the Wee Wee pad whatever you're using. If possible do not even put him down but rather carry him to where his designated bathroom area is. Pick a phrase (Ex. "Go potty) and repeat as your pup is walking around in the bathroom area. I recommend to all my clients to use a leash rather than your hands to keep your puppy either on the pad or in the outside bathroom area. If and when he goes, praise, praise, praise, and treat. Note if this is the first time your puppy goes to the bathroom where you want him to, handstands are allowed! Do not run upstairs to get the treat. Have it with you. Otherwise, the treat is not enforcing what you're praising him about.

7:30 am - Breakfast. Limit the time for him to eat to 30 min.

8:00 am- Back to the bathroom area. Young puppies are like combustible engines. They eat and then it usually goes right through them. If he eliminates, playtime is fine. Remember; do not let your puppy out of your sight. Keep him in a contained area. If you need to do errands, take a shower, have a life, etc. Your little guy must be crated when you're not around.

12:00 pm- Puppy comes out of crate. Back to bathroom area. Use your bathroom phrase (Go potty)

12:30 pm- Lunchtime. Followed by bathroom visit and then playtime with supervision

6:00 pm – Puppy (if not being watched) is taken out of crate, brought over to bathroom area.

6:30 pm- Dinner

7:00 pm- Brought back to bathroom area

7:30-10:00pm- Hanging out with the family. Playing with constant supervision. Consider leaving leash on the puppy during this time to help control nipping, jumping, chewing furniture, etc.

10:00 pm- Bathroom time

10:30 –11:00 pm Night night puppy. See you in the morning.

Chapter Two Summary

- Dogs are considered puppies from birth to about one year of age.
- All puppies are totally dependent on their mothers at birth.
- A newborn puppy will spend 90 percent of its time sleeping only waking to nurse.
- Never adopt or purchase a puppy that is less than eight weeks old.
- You should puppy proof your house.
- Crating the puppy creates a soft warm home and prevents your puppy from engaging in destructive behavior while not being watched.
- By keeping puppy in an enclosed area he will do his best not to go to the bathroom and soil himself or his bed.
- Your puppy won't show his true puppy personality for a good 2-3 weeks after you bring him home.
- Don't expect your new puppy to understand what you want automatically! It takes work, patience, and consistency on our part.

NOTES:

Our Puppy Journal

We brought you home on _____

Your first impressions of your new home were _____
_____
_____
_____
_____

We named you _____

Your favorite toys were_____
_____
_____
_____
_____

(Paste Pictures of Puppy Here)

Chapter Three
The Early School Age Years (3-6 months)

Wait a minute... how did we go from bringing home puppy to school age years? Simple, let me explain. Most folks seem to think that the rule of thumb for understanding their dog's age compared to that of humans is the old 7 to 1 ratio. Meaning every year of your dog's life is equivalent to seven human years. Example: Sparky is 4 years so Sparky would be 4 x 7= 28 years old in human years.

While the whole lucky 7 thing may be easier to calculate in your head, a much more accurate determination of your pooch's age is the following formula:

Year 1 in a dog's life = 16 human years
Year 2 in a dog's life = 12 human years
Year 3 in a dog's life, and onward = 5 human years

So if you do the math, using this more accurate formula Sparky would really be...

16 + 12 + 5+ 5 = 38 in human years!

So what's the big deal? Not much as your dog ages. The big difference is in the first and second years of his life. Now you understand why we say that a 3-6 month old puppy is like a 5-8 year old child in terms of their maturity and development. You may not have to buy him back to school supplies and a fancy lunch box, but nonetheless, this truly is the time that the real learning begins! In fact, your dog will learn more in the next few months than he will in his entire life.

The Energizer Bunny

3-6 months is also the age to begin working with your dog on certain behavior characteristics that need to be discouraged as well as others that should be encouraged. This time is usually referred to as... obedience training. (Maybe he needs a school lunch box after all.)

As your puppy becomes more confident with you and his surroundings, he will become much more active, energetic and curious. This is the age when I usually start getting the phone calls from frantic puppy moms and dads who don't know what happened to their "obedient" 12 week old pup who has somehow transformed into a nonstop never needs to be charged Energizer Bunny that seems to have forgotten everything he knew.

For example, the other day I was talking to someone who was thinking about using me for training their 4 month old Havanese. I was trying to explain to her how one of the most important concepts every puppy mommy and daddy needs to work on with their dogs is recall, or more commonly referred to as the command "come". If you live on 40 acres maybe it isn't so important. There is lots of open space and puppy is safe to roam about. When he gets tired or hungry he will COME home. However, to most city dwellers, this command is imperative to your dog's safety and ability to enjoy their life.

Anyway, my client informed me, that working on this command wasn't necessary because her pup always would come running when she called his name. I explained to her that his dependence on her and his curiosity level would be shifting really soon. His desire to come running to 'mama' when called was most likely going to change. She thanked me and said she would be in touch.

About 4 weeks later, she signed up for dog training. It seems her dog had learned how to venture out from behind momma's apron strings and no longer 'came a runnin' when called. Does it sound bad if I say I had to fight back saying, "I told you so?"

I see this happen all the time. Why? Because it's perfectly natural normal puppy behavior! It is what they do. They must be taught to behave in a different way. There is a saying in the biz, "Don't complain... TRAIN!"

SO BIG

While puppy may not be able to hold his paws stretched up to the sky in a so big gesture, nonetheless he is growing up. Around 4 months puppy will start to lose his puppy fur and get his adult coat. By the end of this early school age phase, puppy will also have attained most of his adult height. And don't be surprised if you happen to see a little drop of blood on puppies chew toy right around now too. Your little baby is losing his milk teeth and adult canine choppers are coming in. Which leads us to our next thing, TEETHING! And what comes with teething? Why it is one of everybody's all-time favorite puppy behaviors. Nipping and Chewing! Yeah I was kidding with the whole favorite thing. Let's just say if you have a favorite pair of shoes or new sunglasses lying around, you might want to move them to where puppy can-not get to them. But don't worry; I have a great training tip at the end of this chapter to help with this!

Time to ALTER Your Opinion and Maybe Your Puppy Too!

While your puppy may be considered the age of a 1st grader, his body is more like that of a pre-teen during this time. In other words, puppy is going through puberty and his hor-mones are all over the place. You may start to experience some very undesirable behaviors. Yes that couch cushion or Uncle Paul's leg may get some unexpected extra attention. Your sweet puppy may start "marking" his territory by spray-ing strong-smelling urine on furniture, curtains, patios, and gardens; basically anything within leg raising reach. Little Romeo may also start to roam, stray away from home in search of his Juliette.

As for females, this can be the time right before they enter their first HEAT (cycle). This cycle last 21 days and happens every six months. Your nice and calm puppy can become, well moody; and if Romeo is not knocking on her balcony door she too may stray to find him!

Many new pet owners want to do the responsible thing, but they just don't really know enough about this whole altering of their pets reproductive systems to make that decision of whether or not it is right for their pet. Having your dog fixed is a very personal decision, and you may have some questions about the advantages or disadvantages to doing so. I am amazed at how much incorrect information there is out there on this subject.

To begin with the terms spayed and neutered are thrown around but perhaps you don't really know what they mean. When a female dog is spayed, the veterinarian usually removes the ovaries, fallopian tubes, and uterus so that she cannot become pregnant. When a male dog is neutered, the veterinarian removes the male's testicles so that he is not capable of getting a female dog pregnant. In both cases, the operation is performed while the pet is under anesthesia so puppy is unable to feel pain. The actual surgical procedure doesn't take that long; however the anesthesia takes a while to wear off. Therefore, your pet will likely have to stay at the vet's office for a few hours, possibly overnight. You will have to keep your pet calm and quiet for a few days so that the incision will have time to properly heal.

Right about now is when my new pet owners usually are shaking their heads and wondering why on earth they would want to put there puppy through all that. There are many advantages to having your dog spayed or neutered. Like do you ever want to take your dog to that fun dog park down the street, to daycare or board him for a night or two so you can have a special anniversary getaway with the spouse? Then your dog needs to be spayed or neutered, as most dog parks, daycares and doggie boarders require it. Research is also now showing that early spaying of female dogs may help protect them from serious health problems such as uterine infections and cancers; and neutering of males can improve their health by reducing the risk of prostate disease, testicular cancer and infections.

You still may not be sure and most likely you have more questions. Below are some of the most commonly asked questions I get and of course, my answers. Read them, talk to your veterinarian and make the decision that is right for you and your dog.

QUESTION: Aren't only MUTTS fixed? My dog is a purebred.
ANSWER: One out of every four pets brought to animal shelters in the United States is a purebred. While you would never abandon your dog, you cannot be a 100% sure that the people who take the puppies wouldn't. (Something to keep in mind.)

QUESTION: Does allowing my dog to have just one litter really matter? It's just one litter of cute puppies that everyone will want.
ANSWER: According to the Humane Society of the United States, 10,000 babies are born in the United States on any given day. On that same day, however, 70,000 puppies and kittens are born. I'm not a mathematician but even I can figure out that those numbers don't match up and that there will never be enough homes for all the animals born.

QUESTION: I heard spaying or neutering will alter my dogs personality is that true?

ANSWER: Any slight changes that may occur will be positive ones. Your puppy will remain a caring, loving and protective companion but will most likely just be calmer. Neutering male dogs also tends to stop their roaming and fighting, and they also lose the desire to mark their territory with urine.

QUESTION: But won't my puppy get fat and lazy if we have him fixed?

ANSWER: Most pets get fat and lazy because their owners feed them too much and don't give them enough exercise, not because they were spayed or neutered.

QUESTION: Isn't it expensive to have my pet spayed or neutered?

ANSWER: Not as expensive as paying for food and care of a litter of puppies. Also many states offer low-cost spay/neuter programs that make the surgery affordable. Many cities also offer reduced licensing fees for owners of spayed and neutered pets. To find a low-cost program near you, call your local humane society or shelter.

Michael's Training Tip Two

Most anthropologists agree that modern dog first emerged somewhere between 10,000-30,000 years ago. Therefore, it stands to reason that there have been billions perhaps trillions of puppies born into the world. Here's the point- every single one of these puppies NIPPED!!! So take heart, you are not alone.

Puppies nip for a variety of reasons: playing, curiosity, and teething. Puppies play with their littermates with their teeth. Just like human babies do, puppies explore by putting everything into their mouth. And once again, just like human babies seek comfort by chewing on a pacifier or mama's finger, puppies do the same thing when they are teething. As your puppy goes through the teething stage (anywhere from 3-7 months) it really is uncomfortable for your little guy; hence the desire to chew on your flip-flops and anything else he can wrap those choppers around.

While chewing and nipping is normal puppy behavior, our goal is to show puppy what is acceptable and what is off limits when it comes to chewing and/or nipping. In all my puppy-training programs, I address this by focusing on 2 key strategies: Redirection and Management.

Redirection

The idea behind redirection is through the use of your voice you will be able to start showing your puppy what is ok to chew and what isn't. Words are not as important as the tone and firmness of your voice is. Telling your sweet little puppy to stop tugging on your shoelaces while chuckling will only encourage that behavior. If you do this, then you certainly cannot blame your dog as he gets older when that cute nipping turns into ripping pants and shirts as well.

Redirection is rather simple once you get the hang of it. When your puppy starts to nip or chew on you, your children, or some other unacceptable object, in a firm voice correct and then re-direct him to the squeaky toy or chewy toy he should chew on. Make sure to praise him when he does start to chew on the acceptable item. Consistency and patience is required for redirection to work.

Another tool is to take a tasty treat your puppy enjoys and close your hand around it. When your puppy licks your hand to get to the treat give him a big praise and allow him to have the treat. If he chews on your hand make a big noise and withdraw your hand. This starts to teach your dog the benefit of "kisses" vs. using his teeth.

Management

This is the harder of the two strategies to implement. There will be times when all the re-direction in the world fails to work and nothing is as much fun for your puppy to chew on than your hand, your shoe, a sock, etc. This typically occurs when your puppy is having his crazy high-energy puppy "happy hours" usually at night or in the morning. This is where you must manage the situation. I recommend keeping a short (4ft.) leash on your puppy in the house and let him run around with the leash on during this time. NOTE: You should only use a leash when your puppy is being watched (which should be all the time) so he does not get hurt. The leash will help immeasurably in controlling the nipping, biting, as well as jumping that are bound to occur. If your puppy knows any commands (such as "sit" or "down") this is a great time to grab the leash and re-direct into one of these and of course compensate with praise and a yummy treat. This will help your dog change his focus from the negative behavior (nipping, chewing, etc.) and reward a positive behavior.

Remember, your little guy is going through a painful teething process. Those new teeth are like razor blades. Help him by giving him cold things to chew on such as a frozen Kong or frozen baby carrots, which are excellent alternatives that really work. Don't forget about the chewy toys too.

The good news is all dogs eventually get through this stage. Hang in there Mom and Dad! Note: If your dog is still nipping at 10-12 months, this is no longer due to teething; but instead is becoming a learned behavior. If this is the case, you may need some professional help from a trainer to help break this bad habit.

CHAPTER THREE SUMMARY

- Year 1 in a dog's life = 16 human years
- Year 2 in a dog's life = 12 human years
- Year 3 in a dog's life, and onward = 5 human years
- Your dog will learn more by the time he is 6 months old than he will in his entire life.
- As your puppy becomes more confident with you and his surroundings, he will become much more active, energetic and curious.
- Around 4 months puppy will start to lose his puppy fur and get his adult coat.
- Adult canine teeth are coming in, which leads to TEETHING.
- Your puppy is starting to reach sexual maturity which means you will need to decide whether or not to spay or neuter her/him.

NOTES:

Our Puppy Journal

At 3 months old you weighed _____.

At 6 months old you weighed _____.

A funny thing you did during this time was

_____

_____

_____

_____

You started to learn commands and tricks like

_____

_____

_____

_____

Your favorite thing to do was

_____

_____

_____

_____

(Paste Pictures of Puppy 3 -6 months here)

CHAPTER FOUR
Off To Work We Go
(6-9 months)

Your little guy may not be so little anymore! Your pup is start-ing to grow up and mature.   At this stage you may actually see a lessening of some of the puppy antics such as nipping and chewing. At the same time, keep in mind; larger dogs take longer to mature. Labs, Golden Retrievers, and other larger breed dogs are just beginning to hit their prime pup-pyhood at 6 months old and really start acting out at this stage.

Puppies between six and nine months are still grow-ing rapidly as they reach their adolescence, or "teenage," phase. They should have all of their adult teeth at this time, and if any baby teeth are retained you should consult your veterinarian for their removal. These remaining baby teeth may appear as a small tooth crowded next to an adult tooth in the same location.

Also, if you haven't done so already, this is the time to spay or neuter your pup. Spaying and neutering can also help to lessen the development of certain behavioral issues in your puppy as he or she continues to grow.

At this age, your puppy should still be eating a diet formu-lated for growing dogs, but you may be able to reduce the number of feedings from three times a day to two meals a day.

By six months, puppies should have completed their full series of vaccinations, which are ideally given at 8, 12 and 16 weeks of age.

The remainder of this chapter will focus on how to actually train your dog. While most people use the term "obedience training" I like to refer to this activity as "communication time." You will simply be communicating with your furry child what is expected of them, what their job is in your family and your home.

Yes you read right, I wrote job! For thousands of years, all dogs had jobs. They were used in hunting, taught to be retrievers; they herded sheep and cattle, pulled carts or sleighs, protected property and guarded valuables and homes. Now, all of a sudden there is no work! Lack of PURPOSE is a dog's worst enemy. We have to give our dogs' gainful employment. They need it. More importantly, they want it and thrive when they have it. Without work, boredom, anxiety, and stress will set in.

But how do we employ our dogs? No you don't have to write him a resume or buy him a little doggie suit for an interview. (Although that certainly would be a cute photo for the memory book now wouldn't it? Sorry I digress.) We can "employ" our canine friends by asking them to do and listen to "commands" and in doing so, they will receive a salary or in the form of treats and/or praise. Whether a dog sits for 30 seconds vs. 60 seconds is immaterial. A perfect "heel", as opposed to a dog that stays from your side a few inches when heeling... does it really matter? NO! The important thing is that you have employed your dog. He is working. He has purpose. The bond of communication becomes stronger and stronger. That's why we ask our dogs to sit, stay, roll over, give paw, etc. The more you work with your dog, the more they enjoy it and look forward to it.

So all dog owners and would be dog owners, hire your dog today, please! Operators are standing by!

Let's Do THIS...

How do we get our dogs to work... we work with them! Clever twist of words there, don't you think? Most, if not all, trainers agree that dogs respond best to positive reinforcement training techniques; with the positive stuff usually being treats and praise. The reason we use treats and praise as reward factors is pretty simple. Most puppies respond to it. However, not every puppy has a high food drive. Some may actually have a high prey drive. This means they love to chase and catch things. In that case, squeaky toys or tennis balls might prove to be the better option to train with. Typically, treats are used as the inducement or "lure" to train with. Once your pup is doing whatever you're asking of him, it can be reinforced with a variety of things such as praise, belly rub, car ride or a nice long walk. Remember, the only time your puppy gets a treat is when they earn it.

Michael's Training Tip Three

The most basic of all training exercises is the sit followed by the sit/stay. While it might seem simple, there are actually different levels of complexity for the sit/stay as well as various uses for it. If you have a dog that loves to bolt out of the front door as soon as it's opened, a strong sit/stay could prove to be a great asset. If your dog is a big jumper and loves to greet everybody by jumping on him or her, a sit/stay could really help.

Teaching the sit and then the sit/ stay is fairly simple. Take a treat in your hand and slowly in an underhand motion lift the treat up and over your puppy's head. Your dog's natural response is to follow your hand with the treat. Causing him to look up and put his butt on the floor. Once that occurs, mark the exercise (NOTE: see separate section a little further down in reference to reward markers.) and treat. Dogs respond better and quicker to non-verbal hand signals than to the word. Eventually they will associate the word "sit" with the action, but initially your puppy will respond to the hand signal we just discussed faster. Once your dog masters the sit, then the next step is to take the same hand and put into a stop-sign position and say, "stay".

The 3 ds of dog training are duration, distance, and distraction. The first "d" duration is what you should concentrate on first. Remember, we are giving our dog a job. So if your puppy can do a sit/stay for 10 seconds today, tomorrow try for 15; the day after that 20; after that 25, etc., etc., etc. Of course, there will be days that your incredibly smart puppy will be off. That's fine; in fact it's rather normal. We all have off days, why should puppy be any different? When it does happen, just back off what you're asking from him in terms of duration and then proceed. We want our puppy to succeed, not fail.

Remember, our dogs learn from being told "yes" not "no". Consistency and patience is the name of the game when it comes to training.

Reward markers- the how and the why

As mentioned previously, when your dog is doing the exercises you are asking him to do, marking the asked for response will greatly improve his learning curve. A marker is something that we as trainers use to "mark" the asked for exercise and tell the dog that something really good is coming. Reward markers help us clumsy humans. Dogs live in the here and now. They don't live in the past or the future. Imagine if we were that fortunate. Think of all the money we could save in therapy bills!!! Since dogs "live in the moment" there is somewhere between 1-2 seconds you as a trainer have to reward your puppy for the exercise he just did. If you are fumbling around for the treat or delayed in giving the praise your puppy deserves for a perfect sit/stay your dog will take the treat, but the association between the sit/stay and the reward is lost. Therefore, to help us we use a reward marker. These reward markers can be a verbal phrase like yes or good job or it can be a sound made by using a clicker. This is the essence of clicker training.

Michael's Training Tip Four

After sit and sit/stay the next exercise to work on is the down and down/stay. Notice the word used is "down". If you constantly correct your dog for jumping up on people and/

or furniture by saying "No Sparky, down" you need to pick a different word for the exercise. Many times I'll be working with a dog and trying to do down and the dog looks at me like I'm talking Martian. Typically, it's because down to this guy does not mean lie down, but rather than stop jumping on Uncle Ted. So he sits there looking at me thinking, "I'm not jumping. What does this fool think I'm doing?" Again, be careful with what words and gestures you use in training.

To teach down to your dog, put your dog into a sit. Then take the treat or the "lure" and slowly bring the treat down to your dog's toes and drag it along the ground, making like an "L". Your dog's response will be to follow the treat with his nose and eventually cause him to lie down in order to get the treat. When then occurs, mark and treat. Once the down is perfected, then start working on the down/stay in the same manner as the sit/stay.

Issues that can occur when teaching the down command

1. Every time I move the treat away from my puppy he stands up.

In order to work with this, first make sure your puppy has a good stay in the sit position. That will help when teaching the down. If your pup knows he can't stand up from the stay and really wants that treat you are slowly extending away from his body, the only way he can get to it is by stretching out in a prone position.

2. No matter how I try, my dog just doesn't get it.

Some puppies have a hard time figuring out what you want when teaching the down. Here is a great technique that works well for dogs that won't go into a down. Get on the floor near your dog. Put him into a sit. Make a tunnel out of one your legs, leaving just enough room for your dog to crawl through. Show him your treat. Give the command down and slowly bring your hand through your leg. If your pup wants the treat, he will have to get in to a down position to crawl under your leg to get the treat. Once he does, mark it and offer the treat. Once your dog is doing the down fairly proficiently, stand up and try the down as you initially tried it.

The goal in the down is to have your dog look at you as you make a downward sweeping gesture with your hand and he lies down. Once this is accomplished, you can proceed to the down/stay.

Michael's Training Tip Five

1. Dogs tend to stay longer in the down than the sit. It's a more natural position for them. It also takes more energy to get up then it takes to stay on the down position.
2. Even though we initially teach the down from a sit position, as your dog advances in his training, start asking him to go into a down from a standing position. Another common mistake is to ask your dog to "sit down." These are two different exercises for your puppy and they should be treated by you as the trainer as such

These represent the first exercises to work on with your dog. There are many more as well as advanced stages of sit and down. After the first "d" duration, then you can precede to the second "d" which is distance and the go on the third "d" which is the hardest of them all, distraction. That's when your puppy can do all that he's learned outside with all types of noises and smells.

You will find the more you ask of your dog, the more he will want to learn. So put you puppy to work and see far the both of you can go.

CHAPTER FOUR SUMMARY

- 6 to 9 months is the age where training is the most effective
- Lack of PURPOSE is a dog's worst enemy.
- Without work, boredom, anxiety, and stress will set in.
- The 3 ds of dog training are duration, distance, and distraction.
- When your dog is doing the exercises you are asking him to do marking the asked for response will greatly improve his learning curve.

NOTES:

Our Puppy Journal

At 6 months old you weighed _____.

A funny thing you did during this time was

_____

_____

_____

_____

You started to learn commands and tricks like

_____

_____

_____

_____

Your favorite thing to do was

_____

_____

_____

_____

(Paste Pictures of Puppy 6-9 months here.)

Chapter FIVE
Adolescence!
(9-12 months)

What can I say about this stage of puppy development, except, buckle up because things are about to get bumpy! Just like human teenagers, your cute little puppy is now entering his awkward years. He or she will start to produce hormones and while he may not roll his eyes and slam doors the way some 2-legged adolescence do; you will start to see some big changes from your 4-legged buddy. Unfortunately... some of those changes are for the worse.

Dogs go through adolescence much earlier than human teenagers. If you have a small breed canine you may have already been experiencing these changes as they can start as early as five months old. With larger dogs it's more likely to be nine or ten months old and will continue until they are two sometimes three years old. Typically speaking, the bigger the dog the slower the development will be.

Signs of Puberty in Canines
While all dogs are different, there are some general signs to watch for to clue you in on the fact that your puppy has hit puberty.

Adolescence! (9-12 Months)

For Males look for:
- ☐ Descent of the testicles
- ☐ Scent Marking (raising his leg {pee} to mark his territory)
- ☐ May start lifting his leg indoors
- ☐ Becomes less friendly
- ☐ More interested in roaming and less interested in obeying
- ☐ Can start challenging other male dogs

For Females look for:
- ☐ Usually starts with first heat cycle
- ☐ Exhibits erratic behavior
- ☐ Moody
- ☐ Lethargic
- ☐ Shows aggression

In addition to the above signs, there are some downright annoying behaviors that are also characteristic of adolescent dogs. These are:

- ☐ Starts inappropriate chewing (furniture, shoes, etc.)
- ☐ Running around like a maniac, has exuberant energy
- ☐ Starts sexual behavior if not spayed/neutered, humping etc.
- ☐ Starts claiming bed or couch areas and growling when you try to move him/her
- ☐ Starts to pee/poop indoors
- ☐ Displays aggressive behavior (towards people or other dogs)
- ☐ Resource guarding

- ☐ Lack of respect and response
- ☐ Lack of focus and concentration (usually noticed during training sessions)
- ☐ Selective "deafness" (doesn't come when called)
- ☐ Guarding-type breeds (German Shepherds, Rottweiler's, Dobermans, etc.) may start to display severe guarding tendencies
- ☐ Destructiveness
- ☐ Manipulative behavior and continually "testing" you
- ☐ Dominance behavior increases
- ☐ May start to challenge humans

Doesn't sound pretty, does it? In fact, sometimes it feels like most of what you managed to achieve through the socialization period has been lost. But don't worry, most of these behaviors will start to diminish as your 'teen' matures and your cute puppy should turn into a well-behaved dog. Just remember to keep up with the training and socialization tips we discussed in past chapters and you will get through these troubled periods just fine.

Tips for Parenting During the Teen Years

Remember, you are not the first puppy parent to go through this. My Great Dane (Clarence) was a total hooligan through his adolescent period but, once he turned two, he was a sweetheart, and still is.

I've found the best way to handle an adolescent dog through this phase of puppy development is to give the dog plenty of daily exercise to drain his energy and continue with positive training sessions daily. Consistency is key at this point, as is routine. If your dog has started chewing, or any other kind of destructive behavior indoors, then I would definitely recommend crate training or at least confining to a small room while you are out. Using Bitter Apple or Yuk is also a good idea to curb chewing furniture, shoes, etc.

If your dog is displaying any aggressive behavior such as growling when you try to move him, or is "challenging" you then you really should consult with a dog behaviorist or certified trainer. Be very careful whom you use for these issues, as any trainer that tells you to "correct" the behavior using punitive methods is likely to cause a bigger problem.

Unfortunately, the teen years are also the time when many dogs are given up to shelters. Try to hold on and work through your puppy's adolescence and recall why you bought your cute puppy in the first place. Remember this is not personal… it's puberty!

Puppy Development and Fear Periods

As if all those physical and behavioral things weren't enough, your poor pooch will also be entering another fear period. During puppy development, puppies go through four of these fear periods. While I can't be specific to the exact age that your puppy will go through these fear periods, as all puppies differ, I can tell you that these times of anxiety and distress usually happen approximately at the following ages:

1. Between 8-10 weeks
2. Between 4 - 6 months
3. About 9 months
4. Between 14 - 18 months

The fear period is a very important part of puppy development. How you handle this difficult period could determine how well centered your dog will be in the future.

What Does a Fear Period Look Like?

As your puppy enters a fear period, he will suddenly become frightened of something that he used to be okay with or ignored. His reaction could be hunched down, shaking, backing away, hiding, running away, or submissively urinating. Or, your puppy could display more pronounced behaviors such as growling, barking, hackles up, or showing teeth. Either way, once you recognize one of these behaviors at the age ranges mentioned before, it would be wise to stop taking your puppy to new places and introducing him to new things for about a week. If possible, try not to schedule any vet appointments during a fear period. Just like in humans, fear and anxiety is very real, and your puppy needs to be able to trust you.

Michael's Training Tip Six

By now, you puppy should be familiar with the basic commands such as sit, stay, down, and come. At this stage, we can start incorporating some of the more difficult exercises. One such exercise is teaching your dog to: heel.

Heeling means that your dog walks closely by your side with their head parallel to your left leg. When you turn, your dog turns with you. When you stop, he automatically sits by your side waiting until you ask him to continue heeling. This exercise is extremely useful when you're in a crowded area and want your dog close to your side instead of at the end of a leash.

The goal is to make heeling a command that your dog can do through an entire walk. Of course, that's assuming he isn't being walked to go to the bathroom. It certainly is a conflict when you're asking your dog to heel and he has to do potty.

The way to start teaching your dog heel is to have him sit next to you on your left hand side. Rather than use the "old-school" teaching technique of putting a choke collar on your dog and basically dragging him around until he figures out to stay close to your side; I'm not kidding, that's how heeling used to be taught. A much more effective and gentler approach is to get a tasty treat, let your dog smell it and then cup it in your left hand. Put the treat right in front of your dog's nose and using the command "heel", start walking with the treat directly in front of your dog's nose. Hopefully, the treat will act as a lure and he will follow your hand. As you walk repeat the word "heel." Initially, after just a few steps stop, ask your dog to sit, and reward him with the treat, telling him, "good heel". Sounds easy, doesn't it? It's not!

First, always start by using your left leg first when you ask your dog to heel. Your left leg becomes your motion leg, meaning that wherever your leg goes, your dog should be right there along the side. When you want to walk away from your dog, after he is in a sit/stay, always lead with your right leg.

To start, try to make an imaginary square or rectangle. With your dog sitting on your left hand side, give the command "heel" and start walking, left leg first. When you reach the end of one side of your imaginary square, make a left hand turn. Keep walking around the square making left hand turns. The reason for this is because it is easier for you to guide your dog using your left leg when your dog is in the inside while making turns. Making right hand turns or doing an about face is much harder for your dog since he has to learn to pick up his speed as you turn to stay even with you.

The more you do this, the more proficient you and your dog will become at heeling. The ultimate goal is to have your dog able to heel off leash. This will take work and dedication, but the result is having your dog able to walk around without a leash.

CHAPTER FIVE SUMMARY

- Dogs go through adolescence much earlier than human teenagers.
- Small breed canines may start adolescence as early as 5 months, where larger breeds usually start at 9 months. Smaller dogs are considered adults by 12-14 months. Larger dogs will take longer with the giant breeds not reaching maturity until close to 3 years of age.
- Most of the annoying naughty behaviors will start to diminish as your 'teen' matures and your cute puppy should turn into a well-behaved dog!
- During puppy development, puppies go through four fear periods.
- How you handle the difficult fear periods could determine just how well balanced your dog will be in the future.

NOTES:

Our Puppy Journal

At 12 months old you weighed _____

A funny thing you did during this time was

_____

_____

_____

_____

You started to learn commands and tricks like

_____

_____

_____

_____

Your favorite thing to do was

_____

_____

_____

_____

(Paste Picture of Puppy 9-12 months here.)

Puppy Development Wrap Up

You may have come to the end of this guide, but this is just a beginning for you and your pup. Raising a puppy is a big commitment and one not to be taken lightly. To make sure your dog grows from just a mischievous little fellow into a family member who is a joy to live with, takes work. But, you are already ahead of the game. By understanding each stage of your puppy's development, you now have a good idea of what to expect, both developmentally and behaviorally.

By reading this guide you now know that by providing your puppy with a stable routine, consistency, positive training, and plenty of socialization along with exercise you are more likely to produce a well-balanced and emotionally stable dog. You are now better equipped to care for your puppy throughout each phase and reduce the risk of developing behavior problems that are hard, or even impossible, to fix later on. After all, it is these periods of a puppy's life that will shape his personality and character. Quite simply, puppy development affects behavior, and behavior molds character.

Raising a puppy is no walk in the park...but as I am sure you will agree; those sloppy kisses, sweet nuzzles and happy wagging tails when you walk into the room make it well worth the effort!

About The Author

Michael Schaier, owner/head trainer of Michael's Pack, is a Certified Professional Dog Trainer. Michael is the author of *Wag That Tail: A Trainer's Guide to a Happy Dog*. He has appeared frequently on News 12 Long Island, *Animal Island*, and FiOS1 Long Island's *Money and Main$treet*. He has also had featured articles in *Long Island Business News*, as well as *Newsday*.

Michael is devoted to working with dogs and learning how humans and canines can live harmoniously through better communication. Under Michael's leadership, Michael's Pack combines positive reinforcement behavior training with patience and understanding.

47513245R00043

Made in the USA
Charleston, SC
12 October 2015